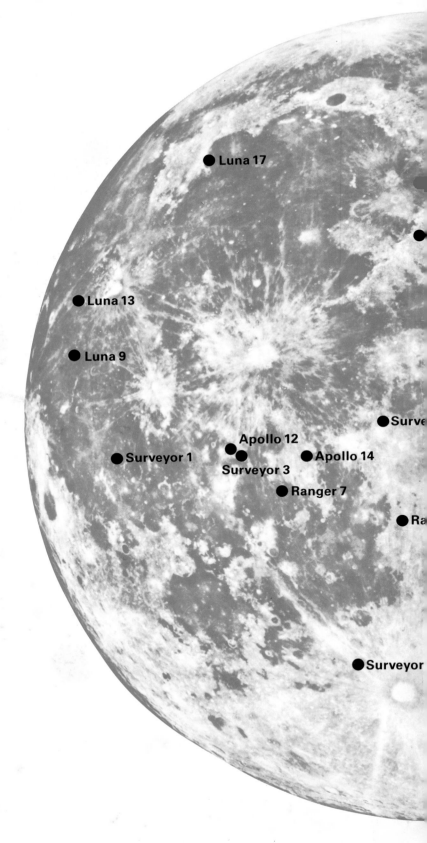

APOLLO (U.S.A.)

APOLLO 11   Launched 16.7.69.
First manned landing on
the moon.

APOLLO 12   Launched 14.11.69.
Second manned moon
landing.

APOLLO 14   Launched 31.1.71.

APOLLO 15   Launched 26.7.71.
First use of Lunar Rover
on the moon.

APOLLO 16   Launched 16.4.72.

APOLLO 17   Launched 17.12.72.
Last manned Apollo
landing on the moon.

SURVEYOR (U.S.A.)

SURVEYOR 1   Launched 30.5.66.
First U.S.A. spacecraft to
work on the moon.

SURVEYOR 3   Launched 17.4.67.
Worked successfully
after a hard landing.

SURVEYOR 5   Launched 8.9.67.

SURVEYOR 6   Launched 7.11.67.
Made 8½ second flight
from the moon.

SURVEYOR 7   Launched 7.1.68.
Last U.S.A. unmanned
flight to the moon.

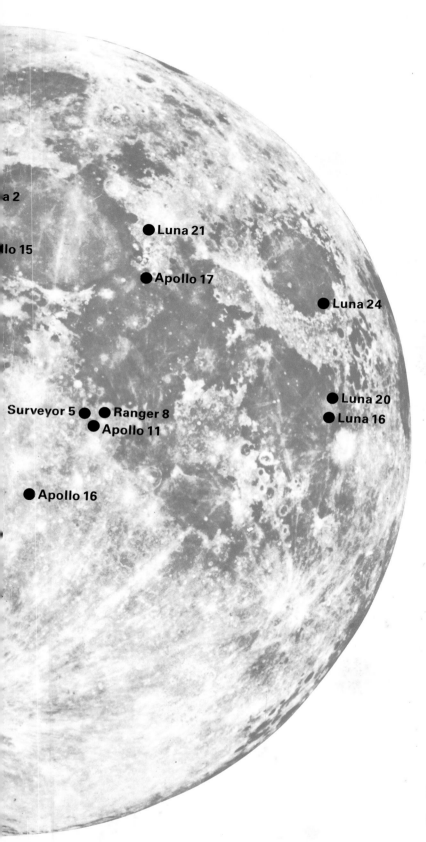

LUNA (RUSSIA)

LUNA 2   Launched 12.9.59.
            First man-made object to
            reach the moon.

LUNA 9   Launched 31.1.66.
            First man-made object to
            work on the moon.

LUNA 13   Launched 21.12.66.
            Second Russian soft lander.

LUNA 16   Launched 12.9.70.
            Returned to earth with
            100 grams of moon soil.

LUNA 17   Launched 10.11.70.
            Landed Lunokhod 1 on
            the moon.

LUNA 20   Launched 14.2.72.
            Repeat of Luna 16.

LUNA 21   Launched 8.1.73.
            Landed Lunokhod 2.

LUNA 24   Launched 9.8.76.
            Repeat of Luna 16.

RANGER (U.S.A.)

RANGER 7   Launched 28.7.64.
            First successful Ranger.
            4000 pictures taken.

RANGER 8   Launched 17.2.65.

RANGER 9   Launched 21.3.65.
            Returned live TV pictures of
            the moon.

First published in 1980 by
Macmillan Children's Books
a division of Macmillan Publishers Limited,
4 Little Essex Street, London WC2R 3LF
and Basingstoke

Published in the United States
by Silver Burdett Company,
Morristown, N.J.
1981 Printing

ISBN 0-382-06615-4

Library of Congress
Catalog No. 81-51496

Designer
Julian Holland
Picture researcher
Caroline Adams
Illustrator
Fred Anderson

Photo credits:
I. M. Ball; California Institution of
Technology and Carnagie Institution of
Washington; European Space Agency;
Geological Museum, London; Lick
Observatory; Matt Irvine; NASA; Novosti;
Photri; Science Museum, London;
Space Frontiers Ltd.
Cover: Space Frontiers Ltd.

Exploration and Discovery

Man and the Moon

John Becklake

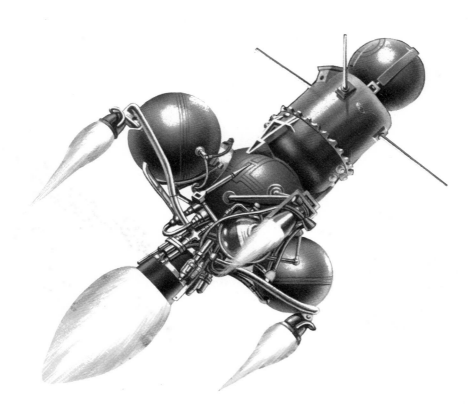

Contents

Left: The Lunar Rover being checked out on the Apollo 17 mission to the moon.

The moon from earth

Above: Cave men must often have wondered about the moon and its changing shape in the night sky.

The moon is the brightest object in the night sky. With our naked eye we can see light and dark patches on it. Some people think that these look like a face – the man in the moon. Early cavemen must have wondered about this strange object. Was it just a light in the sky, or was it another world like earth? Some primitive people worshipped the moon as a god. Later, men tried to explain what the moon might be like. Early astronomers plotted the path of the moon against the stars.

The telescope

However, there is a limit to what we can learn about the moon with the naked eye. The first real step in the exploration of the moon came with the invention of the telescope in the 17th century. In 1609, an Italian scientist called Galileo pointed a telescope at the moon. By today's standards this telescope was very primitive. Yet with it Galileo discovered the craters on the moon. He also saw many hilly regions and large flat areas that he thought might be seas.

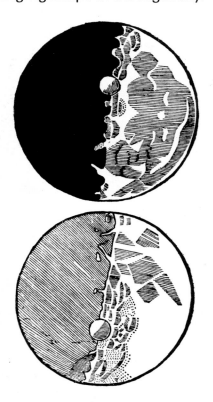

Above: Galileo studied the moon through his telescope. These are the drawings he made of what he saw.

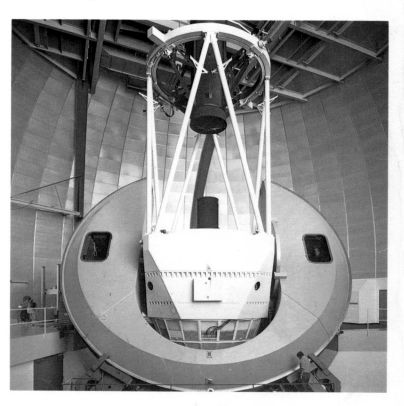

Above: A large modern telescope – this one is at the Kitt Peak Observatory, Arizona, U.S.A. It has a mirror which measures four metres in diameter.

Since then, telescopes have become bigger and more powerful. We have learnt a great deal about the moon's surface with them. Scientists have tried to explain how the craters were formed. Some thought they were caused by meteorites (large pieces of rock from space) crashing into the surface. Others believed they were volcanoes.

By about 1950, scientists had almost reached the limit of their exploration of the moon from earth. Even with the largest telescopes, the smallest object they could see on the moon was about 300 metres wide.

Above: A picture of the full moon taken through a medium-sized telescope. The bright crater at the bottom is called Tycho, after a 16th century astronomer of the same name. The dark areas are fairly flat. The light areas are hilly and heavily cratered. Full moon is not the best time to see the craters because there are fewer shadows than at other times.

5

The moon's path

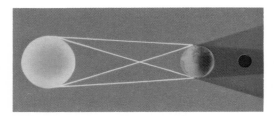

Above: Lunar eclipse. When the earth passes directly between the sun and the moon, it casts a shadow on the moon. This is called an eclipse of the moon. Eclipses of the sun and moon do not happen very often.

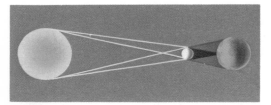

Above: Solar eclipse. Sometimes the moon passes directly between the earth and the sun. Then it casts a shadow on a small part of the earth. Anyone standing in this shadow would see an eclipse of the sun.

The moon and the earth are very different in both size and appearance. The moon is small, rocky and greyish in colour. It has no air and no water and, as far as we know, there is no life on it either.

The moon is only about a quarter the diameter of earth. Its gravity is much weaker. This means that a man on the moon weighs only about one-sixth of what he weighs on earth.

The earth and moon are moving at tremendous speeds through space. They travel around the sun each year at about 107,000 kilometres per hour. At the same time the moon is also moving around the earth. It takes 27.3 days to do this and the same time to turn on its own axis. One moon day lasts slightly longer than this.

We always see the same face of the moon from earth. The earth's gravity is so strong that it holds this side of the moon towards earth. Scientists call this 'captured rotation.'

Below: The earth and moon travel together around the sun. They take $365\frac{1}{4}$ earth days to go around it once. From earth it seems that we are not moving. The moon appears to be travelling around the earth. In fact, the moon is taking a zig-zag path around the sun.

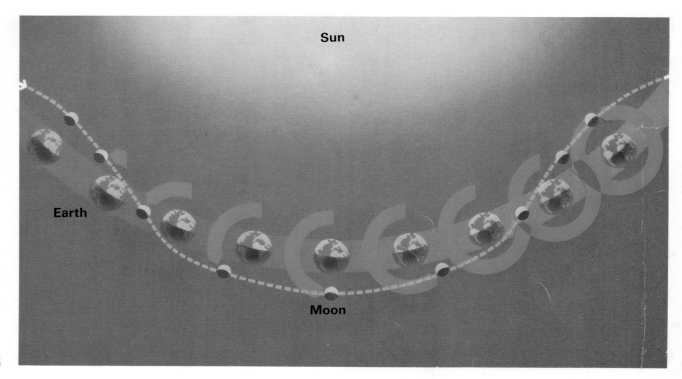

Sun

Earth

Moon

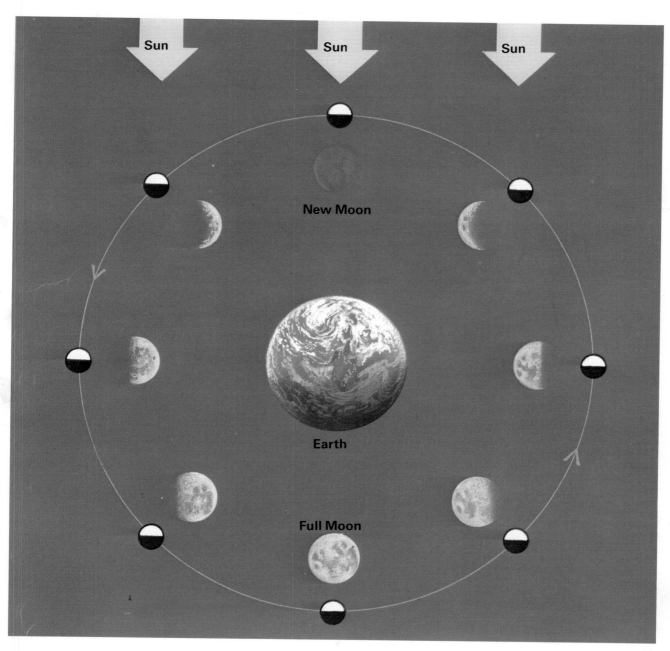

New Moon

Sun

Sun

Sun

Earth

Full Moon

Above: Moonlight is just sunlight reflected from the moon's surface. As the moon goes around the earth, we see different amounts of its sunlit surface. We call these the phases of the moon.

Left: The moon affects our oceans and seas. The strong pull of gravity from the sun and the moon causes high and low tides every day.

7

Fly me to the moon

Above: The moon is 380,000 kilometres away from the earth. This distance is the same as nearly 30 times the diameter of the earth.

Before 1960 no one had travelled faster than 2500 kilometres per hour, and no one had flown more than 40 kilometres above the earth. Yet ten years later two men were standing on the moon 380,000 kilometres away.

Many problems have to be overcome before a man can fly to the moon. One of them is the powerful force of gravity holding us all to earth. To escape from this force we need to accelerate to a speed of 40,000 kilometres per hour. This is 20 times faster than Concorde.

A rocket is the only vehicle we have that can send men to the moon. Men have used firework rockets in war and

Above: A rocket engine being tested on earth.

Left: The German V2 rocket which was used during World War II. It is really the grandfather of today's space rockets.

play for centuries. Modern space rockets, however, are large, expensive, and difficult to make. They have very powerful engines that use a lot of fuel. In fact, when a rocket takes off from the launch pad, more than 90 per cent of its weight is fuel.

In the early days of the space age many of the U.S.A.'s rockets blew up on the launch pad. Since about 1960, they have become much more reliable. Many types of rocket have been built by the U.S.A. and Russia for various space missions. Only one, Saturn V, is powerful enough to send men to the moon.

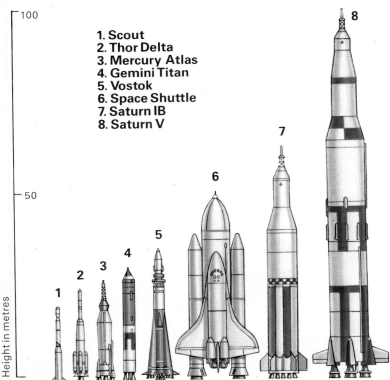

1. Scout
2. Thor Delta
3. Mercury Atlas
4. Gemini Titan
5. Vostok
6. Space Shuttle
7. Saturn IB
8. Saturn V

Height in metres

Above: The rockets in this diagram are all drawn to scale. The giant Saturn V rocket, which took the Apollo astronauts to the moon, towers above them all.

Right: A rocket explodes on the launch pad.

Russia's robot explorers

Above: Sputnik 1, the first man-made satellite.

Below: Luna 9. The small capsule was tossed on to the moon's surface. Then it began taking pictures.

The Space Age began on 4th October 1957. On that day Russia launched the world's first artificial satellite. It was called Sputnik 1. It certainly took the world by surprise. Most people had thought that the U.S.A. would be first to launch a man-made object into space.

In September 1959, another Russian satellite, Luna 2, crashed on to the moon's surface. Then, only a few weeks later, Luna 3 flew round behind the moon taking pictures as it went. This was the first time that man had ever seen the other side of the moon.

Pictures on the moon

The next step was to land a working spacecraft on the moon. On 3rd February 1966, another Russian spacecraft, Luna 9, touched down in the Sea of Storms. It sent back pictures to earth which showed a flat surface with several rocks on it. These were the first pictures ever taken on the moon.

By now the U.S.A. was going ahead with plans to land men on the moon before 1970. Russia, however, seemed to concentrate on using unmanned spacecraft to explore the moon. Luna 16 and Luna 17 were two of these robot explorers.

Below: The first picture of the far side of the moon.

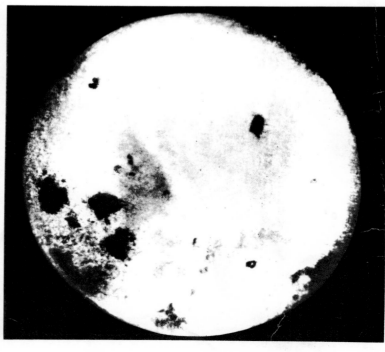

Above and inset: Luna 16. This spacecraft landed on the moon in September 1970. It collected 100 grams of moon soil and placed it in a small capsule on top of the craft. The capsule then lifted off and brought the lunar soil back to earth.

Right: Lunokhod. In November 1970, Luna 17 landed on the moon carrying an eight-wheeled moon buggy called Lunokhod 1. It was really a mobile laboratory controlled by Russian scientists on earth. Lunokhod 1 worked successfully on the moon for nearly a year.

Pathfinders to the moon

We know that early attempts by the U.S.A. to send unmanned spacecraft to the moon failed. We do not know how many failures Russia may have had during the same period. In May 1961, President Kennedy announced that the U.S.A. would land a man on the moon before 1970. Now the 'space race' was really on.

Scientists needed to know a lot about the moon's surface before they could think of sending a man there. Was the surface strong enough to stand the weight of a manned lander? Some scientists thought that the moon was covered with a thick layer of dust that would swallow up any landing spacecraft. The U.S.A. launched three series of unmanned spacecraft – Ranger, Orbiter and Surveyor. They answered these questions.

Ranger (1961 to 1965)

Ranger flew to the moon carrying television cameras. These were switched on some distance from the moon and sent back pictures to earth. As the spacecraft got nearer, they showed more and more detail of the moon's surface. Then it crashed on to the moon.

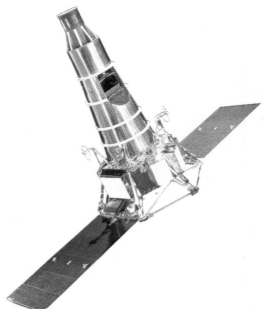

Above: The Ranger Spacecraft. Three of the nine craft were successful. These sent back over 17,000 detailed pictures of the moon.

Below: The Crater Copernicus taken by the Orbiter 2 spacecraft.

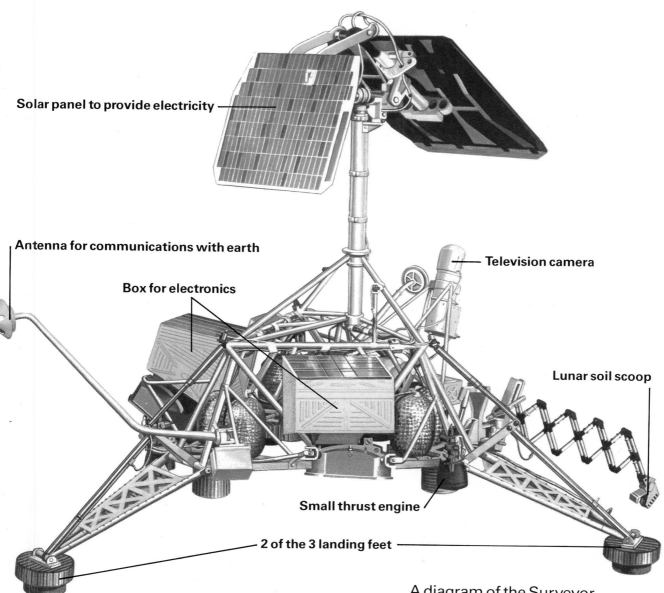

Solar panel to provide electricity

Antenna for communications with earth

Box for electronics

Television camera

Lunar soil scoop

Small thrust engine

2 of the 3 landing feet

A diagram of the Surveyor spacecraft to show its various working parts. The first Surveyor landed on the moon shortly after Russia's Luna 9.

Orbiter (1966 to 1967) and Surveyor (1966 to 1968).
The first three Orbiter spacecraft circled the moon along its equator. They took many photographs of possible landing sites for a manned spacecraft. The last two Orbiters then circled the moon in a different direction. They photographed the rest of the moon's surface.

The Surveyor spacecraft soft-landed on the moon. These were very successful and five of the seven worked as planned. They took over 80,000 pictures of the moon's surface, showing up very tiny particles. They tested the surface and confirmed that it was strong enough to bear the weight of a lander.

Above: The Orbiter spacecraft. They took pictures which showed the best places for a manned landing.

13

How man lives in space

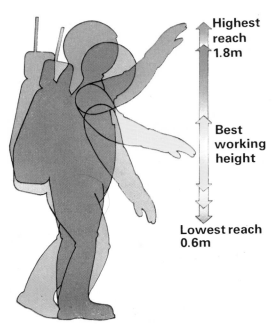

Highest reach 1.8m

Best working height

Lowest reach 0.6m

Above: An astronaut in his spacesuit has limited movement. This diagram shows how far he can reach.

No one can survive in space for more than a few seconds without protection. There is no air to breathe, and our blood would quickly boil because of the very low pressure. In full sunlight the temperature rises to over 100°C. Water boils at this temperature on earth. In the shade it can drop to below −150°C. This is much colder than the bleakest winter on earth. Astronauts are protected from these dangers by their spacecraft and spacesuits.

The spacesuit
When an astronaut leaves his spacecraft, he always wears a spacesuit. He sometimes wears it inside the spacecraft for added safety. The basic Apollo suit has three layers. First there is a comfortable cloth undergarment. Next is a man-shaped nylon balloon. This holds the air that the astronaut breathes. Over this there is a nylon harness to keep the balloon in shape. This basic suit is never worn on its own. It has two different outer garments to protect it.

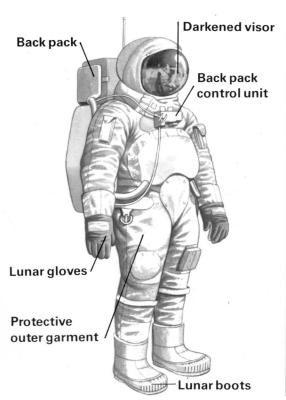

Back pack

Darkened visor

Back pack control unit

Lunar gloves

Protective outer garment

Lunar boots

Above: The Apollo spacesuit, with insulated overboots and gloves, as it is worn on the moon.

Above: Astronaut Ed White wearing his spacesuit as he takes a walk outside Gemini 4 on 3rd June 1965. He was the first U.S. astronaut to walk in space.

An Apollo capsule. Apollo astronauts had pure oxygen to breathe in their cabin. Russian cosmonauts used a normal mixture of oxygen and nitrogen.

A thin outer garment covers the basic suit if it is worn inside the spacecraft. This protects the suit from punctures. Outside the spacecraft, a much thicker outer garment has to be worn. On the moon the astronaut also carries a separate back pack. This supplies him with enough air, pressure and water to last for seven hours.

The spacecraft

A manned spacecraft, such as the Apollo capsule, is built something like a thermos flask. It has an inner and an outer wall. The inner container is sealed and holds the air that the astronauts breathe. The outer wall is thicker and insulates the cabin from the extreme temperatures outside. Part of it is a heatshield several centimetres thick. When the spacecraft re-enters earth's atmosphere, some of the heatshield actually burns away.

Above: An astronaut tries out his position in an Apollo capsule. Space is very limited inside the capsule.

Training for spaceflight

It is very hard to become an astronaut. Even if you are lucky enough to be selected, you still have several years of tough training before your first flight. Every astronaut has to learn about his spacecraft. Everything he will have to do during his flight is practised over and over again on earth.

It is difficult to produce spacelike conditions on earth. Astronauts dressed in spacesuits practice moving around in large tanks of water. They are hung from wires which take most of their weight. This shows them what it will be like to walk on the moon. The astronauts are spun at high speeds on the end of a long arm. This trains them to withstand the tremendous forces at take-off.

Simulated spaceflights

Most important of all, the astronauts practise flying their spacecraft. Complete flights are made on earth in models called simulators. Everything is made as realistic as possible. Rocket noises are fed in over loudspeakers. The astronauts carry out all the tasks of a real spaceflight.

Above: An astronaut in his spacesuit practises laying out lunar surface experiments on earth.

Above: Astronaut training was not always very safe. This lunar landing training vehicle went out of control. The pilot baled out successfully.

Above: Astronauts training in weightless conditions that occur in certain aircraft manoeuvres.

Above: Astronauts train in a large tank of water to teach them how it will feel to be weightless.

Above: Eating in space. Food is mixed with water and squeezed into the mouth from a tube.

Astronauts carry all the food they need into space with them. In space, everything is weightless. This causes problems with eating and drinking. Water does not stay in a cup but floats around in droplets. The astronauts drink by squirting water into their mouths.

Crumbs drifting around in the cabin could cause problems. The first U.S. astronauts ate dried food in bite-sized chunks. They could also mix powdered food with water in a plastic bag to form a paste. They would squeeze this into their mouths. Today's astronauts are better off. They eat special sticky food that sticks to the plate and spoon.

Medical effects

Before man flew in space, doctors were afraid that weightlessness might damage his health. So far, however, no lasting ill effects have been found. A check is kept on the astronauts' health while they are in space. Small detectors are taped to their bodies. These measure their heartbeats, pulse and so on. Many astronauts suffer from spacesickness, like seasickness, early in their flights. This problem does not last for long, however.

The first men in space

The first man to fly in space was Russia's Yuri Gagarin. On 12th April 1961, he flew once around the earth in his Vostok 1 spacecraft. He travelled 40,000 kilometres in just one hour and 48 minutes. It was less than four years since the launch of Sputnik 1, the first artificial satellite.

The first U.S. astronaut to orbit the earth was John Glenn in a Mercury spacecraft in February 1962. The first woman in space was Valentina Tereshkova. She spent three days in orbit in June 1963.

The next step was to fly spacecraft with more than one person on board. In October 1964 Russia squeezed three cosmonauts into Voskhod 1. On the Voskhod 2 flight, Alexi Leonov left his cabin. He became the first man to walk in space.

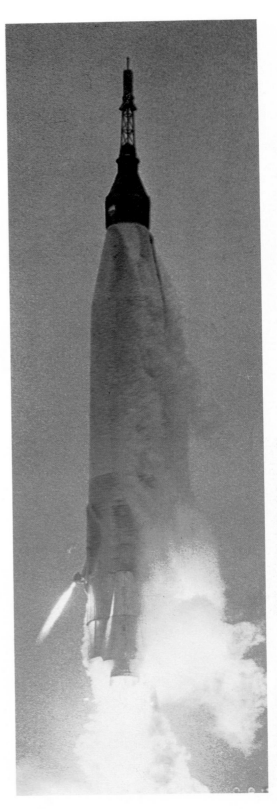

Above: Major Yuri Gagarin – the world's first spaceman. He was killed in an aircraft crash in 1968.

The U.S.A. began the two-man Gemini missions in March 1965. Unlike Russian cosmonauts, the Gemini astronauts could control the flight of their spacecraft. They practised many of the tasks necessary for a manned landing on the moon.

On Gemini 4, Ed White became the first American to walk in space. Another important exercise was for two spacecraft to dock (join up) in space. Gemini 6 approached close to Gemini 7 as they orbited the earth. Then Gemini 8 docked successfully with another unmanned spacecraft in orbit.

Above: An Atlas rocket like this one launched the first American into orbit on 20th February 1962.

Then, early in 1967, disaster struck both the U.S. and Russian space programmes. Fire swept through the cabin of an Apollo spacecraft when it was being tested on earth. All three astronauts in it were killed. The first flight of Russia's new manned spacecraft, Soyuz, also ended in tragedy. On its return to earth the braking parachutes failed. The spacecraft crashed to earth killing cosmonaut Vladimir Komarov.

Manned spaceflights were stopped for 18 months. Careful investigations were made. Then both countries resumed their flights in October 1968.

Early Apollo missions

The U.S.A.'s early Apollo missions all worked successfully. Apollo 7, the first manned Apollo flight, stayed in earth orbit. Apollo 8 took man on his first flight around the moon. Apollo 9 practised docking with the Lunar Module. Finally, in May 1969, Apollo 10 carried out the dress rehearsal for the manned landing on the moon.

Above: The burnt-out cabin of the Apollo capsule. Three astronauts died in the fire.

Above: Astronaut David Scott standing in the open hatch of the Apollo capsule during the flight of Apollo 9. You can see the earth in the background.

Above: The Gemini 6 spacecraft travelling close behind Gemini 7 during their flight in December 1965. 19

Flight to the moon

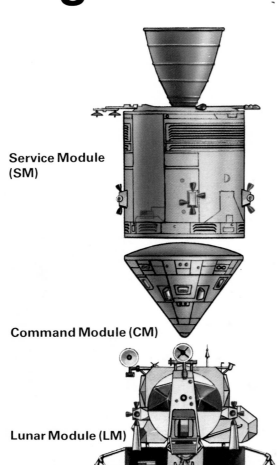

Service Module (SM)

Command Module (CM)

Lunar Module (LM)

The Saturn V rocket lifts the Apollo capsule and its three passengers into orbit around the earth. Then the third stage engine re-fires to send Apollo to the moon.

Next the astronauts fly the Apollo Command and Service Module (CSM) clear of the rocket. The CSM then turns round to collect the Lunar Module (LM). About three days later the complete Apollo spacecraft enters a lunar orbit. Two of the astronauts move into the LM. This undocks from the CSM and descends to the moon's surface. The third astronaut stays behind in the CSM in orbit.

At the end of their stay on the moon, the top part of the LM brings the astronauts back up to the CSM. The LM is then jettisoned (thrown away). The engine in the Service Module (SM) is fired to send Apollo back to earth. Just before it reaches our atmosphere, the SM is also jettisoned. The capsule hits the atmosphere, heatshield first. Parachutes open to lower the capsule into the sea.

Left: The Apollo Lunar Spacecraft. The astronauts' cabin is in the CM. The LM takes two astronauts down to the moon. The SM carries equipment for the CM.

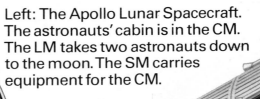

First stage engines

First stage

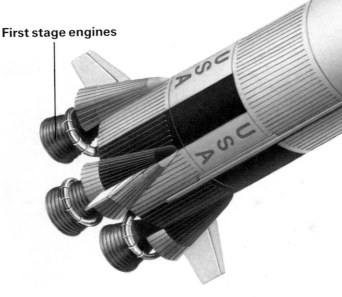

Above: The Saturn V rocket. This three-stage rocket was used on all the Apollo flights to the moon. It is the biggest rocket ever built and it weighs 3000 tonnes at launch. It is 110 metres tall, about the same height as a 36-storey building. Its five first-stage engines are as powerful as 160 Jumbo jet engines.

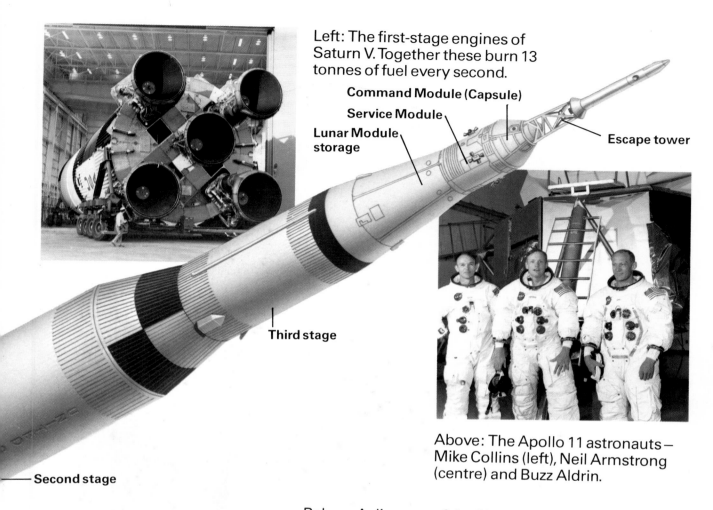

Left: The first-stage engines of Saturn V. Together these burn 13 tonnes of fuel every second.

Command Module (Capsule)

Service Module

Lunar Module storage

Escape tower

Third stage

Second stage

Above: The Apollo 11 astronauts — Mike Collins (left), Neil Armstrong (centre) and Buzz Aldrin.

Below: A diagram of the flight plan used on the Apollo missions to land men on the moon. The spacecraft orbits the earth before setting off for the moon.

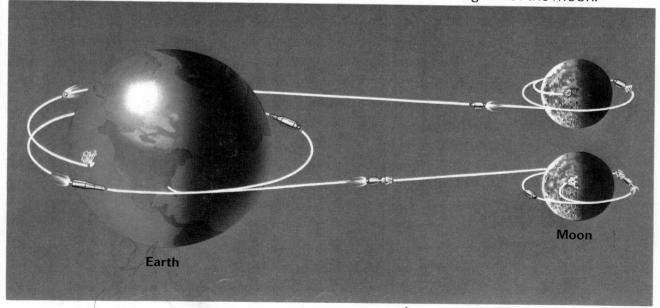

Earth

Moon

Eagle has landed

Above: The launch of Apollo 11 from Cape Canaveral, Florida, U.S.A. One million people were there to see it.

Man's most exciting voyage of exploration began on 16th July 1969. Apollo 11, with astronauts Neil Armstrong, Buzz Aldrin and Mike Collins, set off for the moon. Eagle, the Lunar Module, touched down in the Sea of Tranquillity on 20th July 1969. Armstrong and Aldrin were the two astronauts on board. Collins stayed in lunar orbit in Columbia, the CSM. At 0256 hours Greenwich Mean Time on 21st July 1969, Armstrong stepped off Eagle's ladder. He became the first man to stand on the moon. His first action was to pick up some moon rock.

Then Aldrin came out to join Armstrong. They placed some scientific experiments on the moon and collected more moon rocks. After nearly three hours on the surface they climbed back into Eagle. Twenty-one hours after landing, Eagle carried them back to Columbia.

Splashdown

Apollo 11 splashed down in the Pacific Ocean on 24th July 1969. The two men had spent 22 hours on the moon and brought back 22 kilograms of moon rock. Later missions would stay longer. But the names of Armstrong, Aldrin and Collins will be remembered alongside the great explorers of the past.

Above: Aldrin standing beside the U.S. flag at Tranquillity Base — man's first base on the moon. The astronauts' footprints can be seen in the dust.

Above: Buzz Aldrin climbing down the ladder of Eagle. He was the second man to stand on the moon.

Right: Aldrin against the moon's horizon. You can see Armstrong and the Lunar Module reflected in his visor.

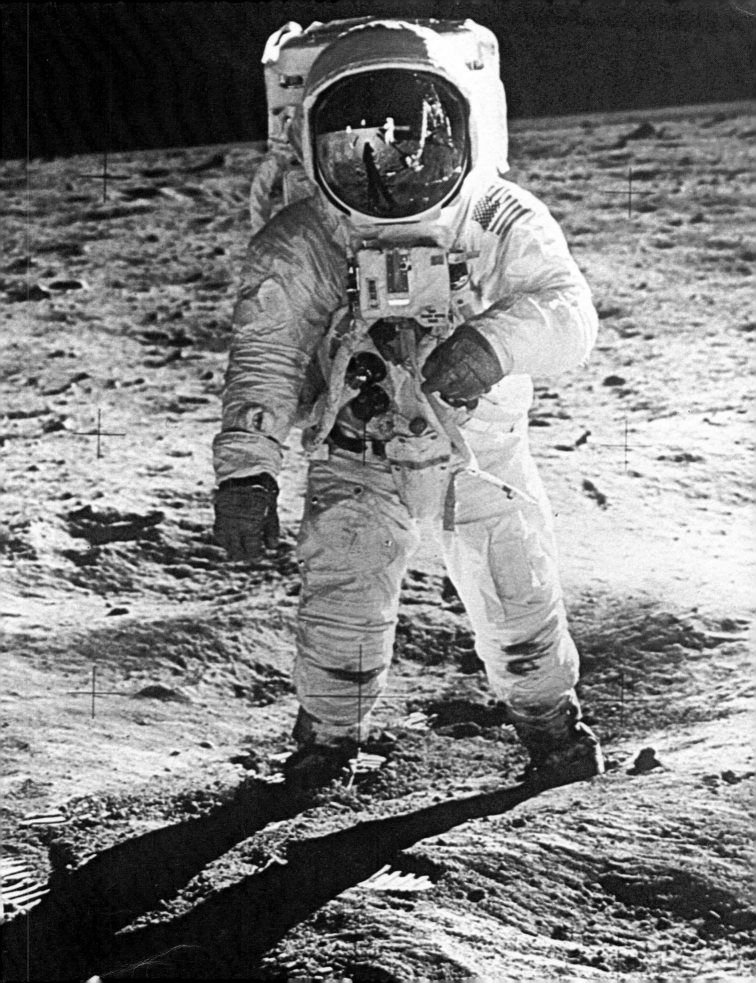

Man returns to the moon

Above: Al Bean looking at Surveyor 3. The Apollo 12 Lunar Module can be seen in the distance.

Below: The Apollo 14 LM photographed from the CSM. The LM has just undocked from the CSM and is on its way down to the moon with its two astronaut passengers.

Apollo 11, the first manned mission to the moon, was a complete success. However, the real exploration of the moon only began with Apollo 12.

Apollo 12

Four months after the first moon landing, Apollo 12 was launched. Despite being struck by lightning at take-off, the Lunar Module, Intrepid, touched down safely on the moon. It landed near Surveyor 3, an earlier unmanned visitor to the moon. Charles Conrad and Al Bean were the two astronauts on board. They placed a package of experiments about 200 metres from Intrepid. They walked for about two kilometres collecting moon rocks. They also took some parts from Surveyor 3.

Apollo 13

Unlike previous Apollo flights, Apollo 13 nearly ended in disaster. It was launched on 11th April 1970 and, at first, all went well. Then, more than halfway to the moon, there was an explosion. The equipment producing electricity for the spacecraft was damaged. Only a small supply of power was left. The moon landing had to be abandoned. The most important thing was to bring the astronauts back safely to earth.

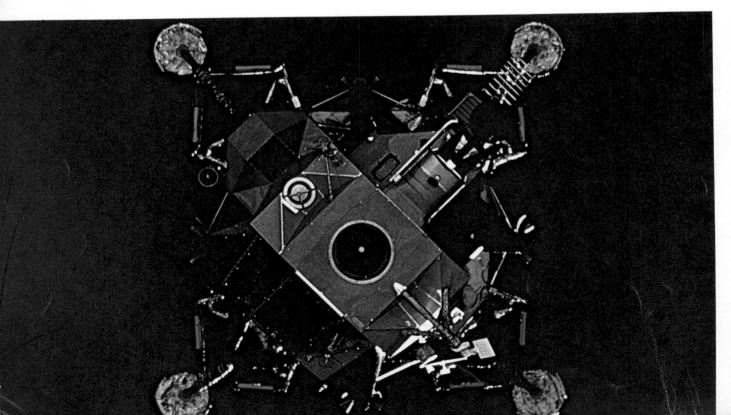

As much power as possible had to be saved for the spacecraft's re-entry into the earth's atmosphere. The astronauts moved into the Lunar Module. The CSM, which they normally travel in, was shut down. All electrical devices that were not essential were turned off. This included the heating. The astronauts spent a miserable journey in the cold, cramped cabin of the LM.

However, all ended safely. As Apollo 13 neared earth, the astronauts moved back into the CM. On 17th April they splashed down in the Pacific Ocean.

Apollo 14

Apollo 14, with astronauts Alan Shepard and Edgar Mitchell, landed at Fra Mauro. This was the region that Apollo 13 should have explored. This time the astronauts used a hand cart to carry their equipment. This helped them travel further and collect more rocks. They also left an experimental package on the moon.

On their second moonwalk, Shepard and Mitchell set out to visit Cone Crater, about 1½ kilometres away. The astronauts in their bulky spacesuits found the last part of the walk difficult. On advice from earth they turned back before reaching the crater.

Above: An astronaut unloading experimental packages from the Apollo 12 Lunar Module.

Above: Astronaut Alan Shepard takes his first look around the moon. He has just stepped down from the Apollo 14 Lunar Module.

25

Exploration continues

The last three Apollo missions spent much longer on the moon than the earlier ones. They also carried out many more experiments. They carried enough air, water, food and power in their Lunar Modules to last for more than 70 hours. Apollos 15, 16 and 17 all carried a Lunar Rover Vehicle, an electric-powered moon car.

Apollo 15

Falcon, the Apollo 15 LM, landed near Hadley Rille in July 1971. The Apollo 15 astronauts, David Scott and James Irwin, were the first to use the Lunar Rover on the moon. They drove nearly 28 kilometres.

They placed the third experimental package on the moon. They stayed for nearly three days and brought about 78 kilograms of moon rock back to earth.

Above: Astronaut Schmitt (Apollo 17) beside a large boulder.

Below: James Irwin (Apollo 15) with the first Lunar Rover on the moon. Mount Hadley is in the background.

Apollo 16

Apollo 16 was launched in April 1972. When the spacecraft reached lunar orbit, a fault was discovered in the CSM. The moon landing almost had to be cancelled. However, it was decided to continue, and the Lunar Module carrying John Young and Charles Duke landed safely. Like the Apollo 15 astronauts, Young and Duke drove their Lunar Rover over the moon. They stopped to collect samples and study the surface.

Above: The top part of the Apollo 16 lander lifts off taking the astronauts back to dock with the CSM.

Below right: A helicopter picks up the Apollo 17 astronauts.

Apollo 17

This was the last Apollo flight to the moon. It was the only one to be launched at night. Apollo 17 landed at Taurus-Littrow on 11th December 1972. Astronaut Harrison Schmitt was the first geologist on the moon.

The work of Apollo

People all over the world have read about the Apollo expeditions to the moon. They have looked at photographs and films of the astronauts walking on the moon's surface. However, most people do not know so much about the important scientific work that was carried out on these expeditions.

The Apollo astronauts placed about 50 experiments on the moon. Many more were carried out on the journeys to and from the moon and in lunar orbit. Most of the experiments were designed to study the moon but some were concerned with medical science.

Moonquake detectors

Several machines to detect moonquakes were left on the moon. These were operated by atomic batteries. They continued to send results back to earth long after the astronauts had left. Many small moonquakes have been detected but they are much less powerful than some of the ones we get on earth.

One of the most important tasks of the Apollo astronauts was to collect moon rocks and bring them back to earth. These rocks are still being studied by scientists all over the world.

Above: The Apollo 15 CSM. Scientific experiments were stored in one side of it and they operated as it circled in lunar orbit.

Above: A piece of moon rock. Altogether over 380 kilograms of moon rock have been brought back to earth by the Apollo astronauts.

Right: An Apollo astronaut collects moon rock with a lunar rake.

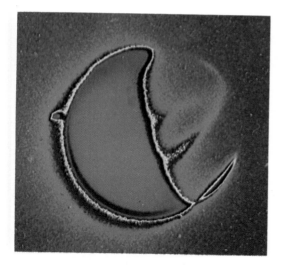

We have learnt from them that the moon is about the same age as the earth – about 4600 million years old. We also know that for the first 1500 million years the moon was bombarded with huge meteorites. At that time too there were active volcanoes on the moon and lava flooded the plains. Scientists have learnt a lot about the moon from the Apollo experiments. They have also discovered that there is a lot more to find out.

Left: A new view of earth from the moon. This picture was taken with an ultra-violet camera from Apollo 16.

Below: Aldrin (Apollo 11) placing a solar wind experiment on the moon. It was used to study the sun.

The future

No man has set foot on the moon since the Apollo 17 astronauts left on 14th December 1972. There are no plans for him to return there in the near future. The Apollo flights were very expensive. The mighty Saturn V rockets could only be used for one launch each.

In an attempt to reduce the enormous cost, the U.S.A. has built a new space launcher. This is called the Space Shuttle and it can be used many times. The Shuttle looks like an aircraft and can carry astronauts and scientists into space. At the end of each flight, it glides back to earth and lands on a runway like a normal aircraft.

One day man will certainly return to the moon. We will build scientific stations and cities there. It is also probable that we will have mines on the moon. These would supply man with vital raw materials.

Our earth in space

The Apollo missions have taught us many things about the moon. They have also helped us to appreciate our own earth more than ever before. From the moon, the earth appears as a beautiful, blue and white planet. In the Universe, it is just another small planet. But the earth is the only place we know where we can live without protection. We must take good care of it.

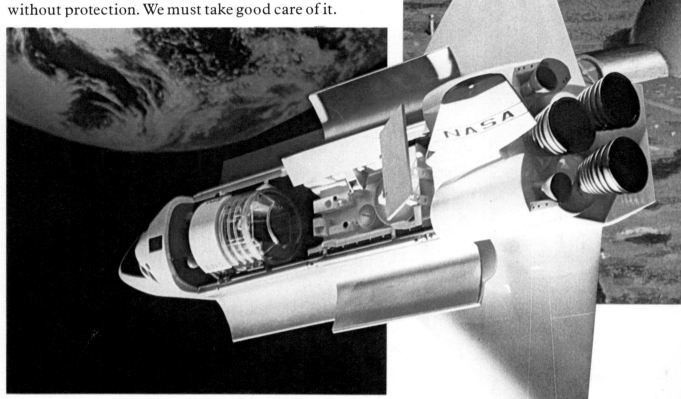

Left: A cutaway picture of the Space Shuttle above the earth. It has a cargo bay 18 metres long. It can carry nearly 30 tonnes of equipment into orbit.

Above: An artist's impression of a manned moon base. It is probable that one day men and women will live and work on the moon for long periods at a time.

Apollo missions to the moon

Spacecraft	Mission dates	Crew	Time spent on moon	Remarks
Apollo 11	16.7.69 to 24.7.69	N. Armstrong E. Aldrin M. Collins	22 hours	First manned landing on moon. Neil Armstrong is the first man to walk on the moon. Brought back 22 kg of moon rock.
Apollo 12	14.11.69 to 24.11.69	C. Conrad A. Bean R. Gordon	32 hours	Second landing on the moon. Brought back 35 kg of moon rock plus bits from Surveyor 3 spacecraft.
Apollo 13	11.4.70 to 17.4.70	J. Lovell F. Haise J. Swigert	None	Moon landing prevented by an explosion in the Service Module.
Apollo 14	31.1.71 to 9.2.71	A. Shepard E. Mitchell S. Roosa	34 hours	First manned visit to the highlands of the moon. Brought back 42 kg of moon rock.
Apollo 15	26.7.71 to 7.8.71	D. Scott J. Irwin A. Worden	67 hours	First of the long stay Apollo missions. First use of the lunar rover. Brought back about 78 kg of moon rock.
Apollo 16	16.4.72 to 27.4.72	J. Young C. Duke T. Mattingly	71 hours	The second use of the lunar rover. Drove 27 km over the moon. Brought back about 98 kg of moon rock.
Apollo 17	7.12.72 to 19.12.72	E. Cernan H. Schmitt R. Evans	76 hours	Last Apollo mission to the moon. First geologist, Schmitt, on the moon. Brought back 115 kg of moon rock.

Left: Eagle, the Apollo 11 Lunar Module, on its ascent from the moon, with astronauts Armstrong and Aldrin on board. The third astronaut, Mike Collins, took this picture from the Command Module where he had remained in lunar orbit. You can see the earth in the background.

Index

APOLLO (U.S.A.)

APOLLO 11   Launched 16.7.69.
First manned landing on
the moon.

APOLLO 12   Launched 14.11.69.
Second manned moon
landing.

APOLLO 14   Launched 31.1.71.

APOLLO 15   Launched 26.7.71.
First use of Lunar Rover
on the moon.

APOLLO 16   Launched 16.4.72.

APOLLO 17   Launched 17.12.72.
Last manned Apollo
landing on the moon.

SURVEYOR (U.S.A.)

SURVEYOR 1   Launched 30.5.66.
First U.S.A. spacecraft to
work on the moon.

SURVEYOR 3   Launched 17.4.67.
Worked successfully
after a hard landing.

SURVEYOR 5   Launched 8.9.67.

SURVEYOR 6   Launched 7.11.67.
Made $8\frac{1}{2}$ second flight
from the moon.

SURVEYOR 7   Launched 7.1.68.
Last U.S.A. unmanned
flight to the moon.

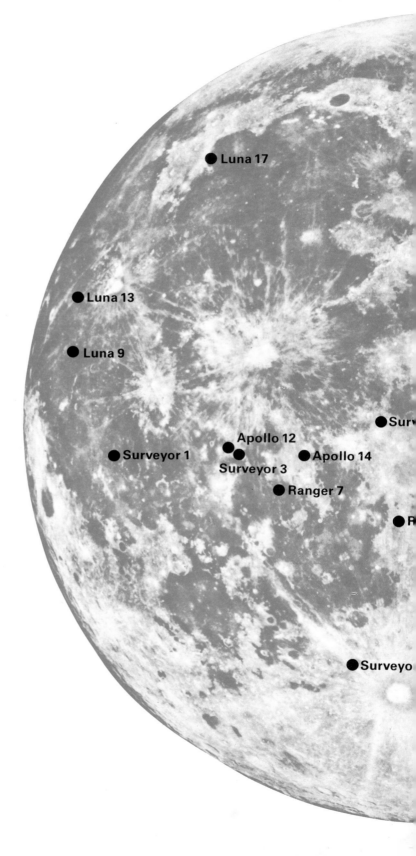

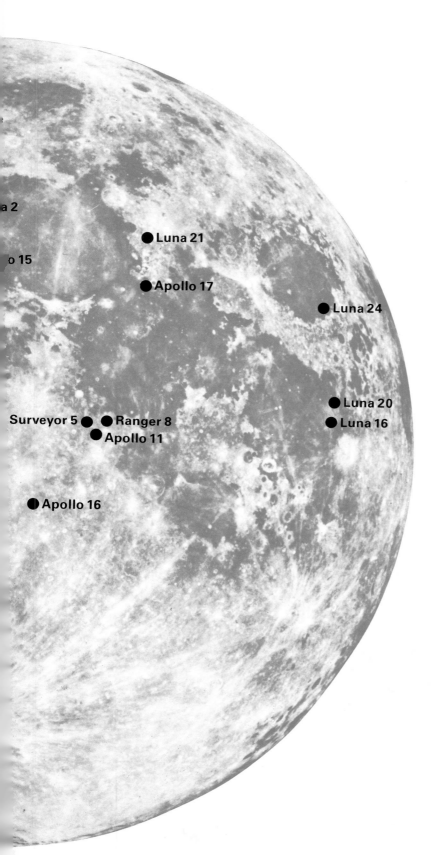

LUNA (RUSSIA)

LUNA 2   Launched 12.9.59.
First man-made object to
reach the moon.

LUNA 9   Launched 31.1.66.
First man-made object to
work on the moon.

LUNA 13   Launched 21.12.66.
Second Russian soft lander.

LUNA 16   Launched 12.9.70.
Returned to earth with
100 grams of moon soil.

LUNA 17   Launched 10.11.70.
Landed Lunokhod 1 on
the moon.

LUNA 20   Launched 14.2.72.
Repeat of Luna 16.

LUNA 21   Launched 8.1.73.
Landed Lunokhod 2.

LUNA 24   Launched 9.8.76.
Repeat of Luna 16.

RANGER (U.S.A.)

RANGER 7   Launched 28.7.64.
First successful Ranger.
4000 pictures taken.

RANGER 8   Launched 17.2.65.

RANGER 9   Launched 21.3.65.
Returned live TV pictures of
the moon.

1 2 3 4 5 6 7 8—U—88 87 86 85 84 83 82 81